Copyright © 2020 Guava Jelly Planners

All rights reserved. No part of this book may be reproduced in any form or by any electronic or mechanical means, including information storage and retrieval systems, without permission in writing from the publisher.

Content & Design by: Guava Jelly Planners. Commercial rights to all fonts and images.

2020 Planner

2020

January
S	M	T	W	T	F	S
			1	2	3	4
5	6	7	8	9	10	11
12	13	14	15	16	17	18
19	20	21	22	23	24	25
26	27	28	29	30	31	

February
S	M	T	W	T	F	S
						1
2	3	4	5	6	7	8
9	10	11	12	13	14	15
16	17	18	19	20	21	22
23	24	25	26	27	28	29

March
S	M	T	W	T	F	S
1	2	3	4	5	6	7
8	9	10	11	12	13	14
15	16	17	18	19	20	21
22	23	24	25	26	27	28
29	30	31				

April
S	M	T	W	T	F	S
			1	2	3	4
5	6	7	8	9	10	11
12	13	14	15	16	17	18
19	20	21	22	23	24	25
26	27	28	29	30		

May
S	M	T	W	T	F	S
					1	2
3	4	5	6	7	8	9
10	11	12	13	14	15	16
17	18	19	20	21	22	23
24	25	26	27	28	29	30
31						

June
S	M	T	W	T	F	S
	1	2	3	4	5	6
7	8	9	10	11	12	13
14	15	16	17	18	19	20
21	22	23	24	25	26	27
28	29	30				

July
S	M	T	W	T	F	S
			1	2	3	4
5	6	7	8	9	10	11
12	13	14	15	16	17	18
19	20	21	22	23	24	25
26	27	28	29	30	31	

August
S	M	T	W	T	F	S
						1
2	3	4	5	6	7	8
9	10	11	12	13	14	15
16	17	18	19	20	21	22
23	24	25	26	27	28	29
30	31					

September
S	M	T	W	T	F	S
		1	2	3	4	5
6	7	8	9	10	11	12
13	14	15	16	17	18	19
20	21	22	23	24	25	26
27	28	29	30			

October
S	M	T	W	T	F	S
				1	2	3
4	5	6	7	8	9	10
11	12	13	14	15	16	17
18	19	20	21	22	23	24
25	26	27	28	29	30	31

November
S	M	T	W	T	F	S
1	2	3	4	5	6	7
8	9	10	11	12	13	14
15	16	17	18	19	20	21
22	23	24	25	26	27	28
29	30					

December
S	M	T	W	T	F	S
		1	2	3	4	5
6	7	8	9	10	11	12
13	14	15	16	17	18	19
20	21	22	23	24	25	26
27	28	29	30	31		

My Wellness Action Plan for 2020

Month:	Action:
January	
February	
March	
April	
May	
June	
July	
August	
September	
October	
November	
December	

Notes

January 2020

Sunday	Monday	Tuesday	Wednesday	Thursday	Friday	Saturday
29	30	31	1 NEW YEAR'S DAY	2	3	4
5	6 EPIPHANY	7	8	9	10	11
12	13	14	15	16	17	18
19	20 MARTIN LUTHER KING DAY (U.S.)	21	22	23	24	25 CHINESE/LUNAR NEW YEAR
26	27	28	29	30	31	1

December

12/30/19 to 01/05/20

○ 30. MONDAY

Goals:

○ 31. TUESDAY

○ 1. WEDNESDAY

Action Steps:

○ 2. THURSDAY

○ 3. FRIDAY

○ 4. SATURDAY/5. SUNDAY

January

01/06/20 to 01/12/20

○ 6. MONDAY

○ 7. TUESDAY

○ 8. WEDNESDAY

○ 9. THURSDAY

○ 10. FRIDAY

○ 11. SATURDAY/ 12. SUNDAY

Goals:

Action Steps:

January

01/13/20 to 01/19/20

○ 13. MONDAY

○ 14. TUESDAY

○ 15. WEDNESDAY

○ 16. THURSDAY

○ 17. FRIDAY

○ 18. SATURDAY / 19. SUNDAY

Goals:

Action Steps:

January

01/20/20 to 01/26/20

○ 20. MONDAY

○ 21. TUESDAY

○ 22. WEDNESDAY

○ 23. THURSDAY

○ 24. FRIDAY

○ 25. SATURDAY / 26. SUNDAY

Goals:

Action Steps:

January

01/27/20 to 02/02/20

○ 27. MONDAY

○ 28. TUESDAY

○ 29. WEDNESDAY

○ 30. THURSDAY

○ 31. FRIDAY

○ 1. SATURDAY / 2. SUNDAY

Goals:

Action Steps:

February 2020

Sunday	Monday	Tuesday	Wednesday	Thursday	Friday	Saturday
26	27	28	29	30	31	1
2	3	4	5	6	7	8
9	10	11	12	13	14 *VALENTINE'S DAY*	15
16	17 *PRESIDENT'S DAY U.S./ FAMILY DAY - CAN*	18	19	20	21	22
23	24	25	26 *ASH WEDNESDAY*	27	28	29

February

02/03/20 to 02/09/20

○ 3. MONDAY

○ 4. TUESDAY

○ 5. WEDNESDAY

○ 6. THURSDAY

○ 7. FRIDAY

○ 8. SATURDAY / 9. SUNDAY

Goals:

Action Steps:

February

02/10/20 to 02/16/20

○ 10. MONDAY

○ 11. TUESDAY

○ 12. WEDNESDAY

○ 13. THURSDAY

○ 14. FRIDAY

○ 15. SATURDAY / 16. SUNDAY

Goals:

Action Steps:

February

02/17/20 to 02/23/20

○ 17. MONDAY

○ 18. TUESDAY

○ 19. WEDNESDAY

○ 20. THURSDAY

○ 21. FRIDAY

○ 22. SATURDAY/23. SUNDAY

Goals:

Action Steps:

February

02/24/20 to 03/01/20

○ 24. MONDAY

○ 25. TUESDAY

○ 26. WEDNESDAY

○ 27. THURSDAY

○ 28. FRIDAY

○ 29. SATURDAY / 1. SUNDAY

Goals:

Action Steps:

March 2020

Sunday	Monday	Tuesday	Wednesday	Thursday	Friday	Saturday
1	2	3	4	5	6	7
8 **DAYLIGHT SAVINGS TIME**	9	10 **PURIM**	11	12	13	14
15	16	17 **ST. PATRICK'S DAY**	18	19	20 **SPRING EQUINOX**	21
22	23	24	25	26	27	28
29	30	31	1	2	3	4

March

03/02/20 to 03/08/20

○ 2. MONDAY

○ 3. TUESDAY

○ 4. WEDNESDAY

○ 5. THURSDAY

○ 6. FRIDAY

○ 7. SATURDAY / 8. SUNDAY

Goals:

Action Steps:

March

03/09/20 to 03/15/20

○ 9. MONDAY

○ 10. TUESDAY

○ 11. WEDNESDAY

○ 12. THURSDAY

○ 13. FRIDAY

○ 14. SATURDAY / 15. SUNDAY

Goals:

Action Steps:

March

03/16/20 to 03/22/20

○ 16. MONDAY

○ 17. TUESDAY

Goals:

○ 18. WEDNESDAY

Action Steps:

○ 19. THURSDAY

○ 20. FRIDAY

○ 21. SATURDAY / 22. SUNDAY

March

03/23/20 to 03/29/20

○ 23. MONDAY

○ 24. TUESDAY

○ 25. WEDNESDAY

○ 26. THURSDAY

○ 27. FRIDAY

○ 28. SATURDAY / 29. SUNDAY

Goals:

Action Steps:

March

03/30/20 to 04/05/20

○ 30. MONDAY

○ 31. TUESDAY

○ 1. WEDNESDAY

○ 2. THURSDAY

○ 3. FRIDAY

○ 4. SATURDAY / 5. SUNDAY

Goals:

Action Steps:

April 2020

Sunday	Monday	Tuesday	Wednesday	Thursday	Friday	Saturday
29	30	31	1	2	3	4
5 **PALM SUNDAY**	6	7	8	9 **JEWISH PASSOVER**	10 **GOOD FRIDAY**	11
12 **EASTER SUNDAY**	13 **EASTER MONDAY**	14	15	16	17	18
19 **ORTHODOX EASTER SUNDAY**	20	21	22 **ADMIN PROFESSIONAL'S DAY**	23	24 **RAMADAN BEGINS**	25
26	27	28	29	30	1	2

April

04/06/20 to 04/12/20

○ 6. MONDAY

○ 7. TUESDAY

○ 8. WEDNESDAY

○ 9. THURSDAY

○ 10. FRIDAY

○ 11. SATURDAY / 12. SUNDAY

Goals:

Action Steps:

April

04/13/20 to 04/19/20

○ 13. MONDAY

○ 14. TUESDAY

○ 15. WEDNESDAY

○ 16. THURSDAY

○ 17. FRIDAY

○ 18. SATURDAY / 19. SUNDAY

Goals:

Action Steps:

April

04/20/20 to 04/26/20

○ 20. MONDAY

○ 21. TUESDAY

○ 22. WEDNESDAY

○ 23. THURSDAY

○ 24. FRIDAY

○ 25. SATURDAY / 26. SUNDAY

Goals:

Action Steps:

April

04/27/20 to 05/03/20

○ 27. MONDAY

○ 28. TUESDAY

○ 29. WEDNESDAY

○ 30. THURSDAY

○ 1. FRIDAY

○ 2. SATURDAY/3. SUNDAY

Goals:

Action Steps:

May 2020

Sunday	Monday	Tuesday	Wednesday	Thursday	Friday	Saturday
26	27	28	29	30	1	2
3	4	5 CINCO DE MAYO	6	7	8	9
10 MOTHER'S DAY	11	12	13	14	15	16 ARMED FORCES DAY
17	18 VICTORIA DAY - CAN	19	20	21	22	23
24 EID AL-TITR	25 MEMORIAL DAY U.S.	26	27	28	29	30
31 PENTECOST DAY	1	2	3	4	5	6

May

05/04/20 to 05/10/20

○ 4. MONDAY

○ 5. TUESDAY

○ 6. WEDNESDAY

○ 7. THURSDAY

○ 8. FRIDAY

○ 9. SATURDAY / 10. SUNDAY

Goals:

Action Steps:

May

05/11/20 to 05/17/20

○ 11. MONDAY

○ 12. TUESDAY

○ 13. WEDNESDAY

○ 14. THURSDAY

○ 15. FRIDAY

○ 16. SATURDAY / 17. SUNDAY

Goals:

Action Steps:

May

05/18/20 to 05/24/20

○ 18. MONDAY

○ 19. TUESDAY

○ 20. WEDNESDAY

○ 21. THURSDAY

○ 22. FRIDAY

○ 23. SATURDAY / 24. SUNDAY

Goals:

Action Steps:

May

05/25/20 to 05/31/20

○ 25. MONDAY

○ 26. TUESDAY

○ 27. WEDNESDAY

○ 28. THURSDAY

○ 29. FRIDAY

○ 30. SATURDAY / 31. SUNDAY

Goals:

Action Steps:

June 2020

Sunday	Monday	Tuesday	Wednesday	Thursday	Friday	Saturday
31	1	2	3	4	5	6
7	8	9	10	11	12	13
14 **FLAG DAY U.S.**	15	16	17	18	19	20 **SUMMER SOLTICE**
21 **FATHER'S DAY**	22	23	24	25	26	27
28	29	30	1	2	3	4

June

06/01/20 to 06/07/20

○ 1. MONDAY

○ 2. TUESDAY

○ 3. WEDNESDAY

○ 4. THURSDAY

○ 5. FRIDAY

○ 6. SATURDAY / 7. SUNDAY

Goals:

Action Steps:

June

06/08/20 to 06/14/20

○ 8. MONDAY

○ 9. TUESDAY

○ 10. WEDNESDAY

○ 11. THURSDAY

○ 12. FRIDAY

○ 13. SATURDAY / 14. SUNDAY

Goals:

Action Steps:

June

06/15/20 to 06/21/20

○ 15. MONDAY

○ 16. TUESDAY

○ 17. WEDNESDAY

○ 18. THURSDAY

○ 19. FRIDAY

○ 20. SATURDAY / 21. SUNDAY

Goals:

Action Steps:

June

06/22/20 to 06/28/20

○ 22. MONDAY

○ 23. TUESDAY

○ 24. WEDNESDAY

○ 25. THURSDAY

○ 26. FRIDAY

○ 27. SATURDAY / 28. SUNDAY

Goals:

Action Steps:

July 2020

Sunday	Monday	Tuesday	Wednesday	Thursday	Friday	Saturday
28	29	30	1 CANADA DAY	2	3	4 INDEPENDENCE DAY U.S.
5	6	7	8	9	10	11
12	13	14	15	16	17	18
19	20	21	22	23	24	25
26 PARENT'S DAY	27	28	29	30	31 EID AL-ADHA	1

June

06/29/20 to 07/05/20

○ 29. MONDAY

○ 30. TUESDAY

○ 1. WEDNESDAY

○ 2. THURSDAY

○ 3. FRIDAY

○ 4. SATURDAY / 5. SUNDAY

Goals:

Action Steps:

July

07/06/20 to 07/12/20

○ 6. MONDAY

○ 7. TUESDAY

○ 8. WEDNESDAY

○ 9. THURSDAY

○ 10. FRIDAY

○ 11. SATURDAY / 12. SUNDAY

Goals:

Action Steps:

July

07/13/20 to 07/19/20

○ 13. MONDAY

○ 14. TUESDAY

○ 15. WEDNESDAY

○ 16. THURSDAY

○ 17. FRIDAY

○ 18. SATURDAY / 19. SUNDAY

Goals:

Action Steps:

July

07/20/20 to 07/26/20

○ 20. MONDAY

○ 21. TUESDAY

○ 22. WEDNESDAY

○ 23. THURSDAY

○ 24. FRIDAY

○ 25. SATURDAY / 26. SUNDAY

Goals:

Action Steps:

July

07/27/20 to 08/02/20

○ 27. MONDAY

○ 28. TUESDAY

○ 29. WEDNESDAY

○ 30. THURSDAY

○ 31. FRIDAY

○ 1. SATURDAY / 2. SUNDAY

Goals:

Action Steps:

August 2020

Sunday	Monday	Tuesday	Wednesday	Thursday	Friday	Saturday
26	27	28	29	30	31	1
2	3 **CIVIC HOLIDAY - CAN**	4	5	6	7	8
9	10	11	12	13	14	15
16	17	18	19	20	21	22
23	24	25	26	27	28	29
30	31	1	2	3	4	5

August

08/03/20 to 08/09/20

○ 3. MONDAY

○ 4. TUESDAY

○ 5. WEDNESDAY

○ 6. THURSDAY

○ 7. FRIDAY

○ 8. SATURDAY / 9. SUNDAY

Goals:

Action Steps:

August

08/10/20 to 08/16/20

○ 10. MONDAY

○ 11. TUESDAY

○ 12. WEDNESDAY

○ 13. THURSDAY

○ 14. FRIDAY

○ 15. SATURDAY/ 16. SUNDAY

Goals:

Action Steps:

August

08/17/20 to 08/23/20

○ 17. MONDAY

○ 18. TUESDAY

○ 19. WEDNESDAY

○ 20. THURSDAY

○ 21. FRIDAY

○ 22. SATURDAY / 23. SUNDAY

Goals:

Action Steps:

August

08/24/20 to 08/30/20

○ 24. MONDAY

○ 25. TUESDAY

○ 26. WEDNESDAY

○ 27. THURSDAY

○ 28. FRIDAY

○ 29. SATURDAY/30. SUNDAY

Goals:

Action Steps:

September 2020

Sunday	Monday	Tuesday	Wednesday	Thursday	Friday	Saturday
30	31	1	2	3	4	5
6	7 **LABOR DAY U.S. & CAN**	8	9	10	11	12
13 **GRAND PARENT'S DAY**	14	15	16	17	18	19 **JEWISH NEW YEAR**
20	21	22 **FALL EQUINOX**	23	24	25 **NATIVE AMERICAN DAY**	26
27	28 **YOM KIPPUR**	29	30	1	2	3

August

08/31/20 to 09/06/20

○ 31. MONDAY

○ 1. TUESDAY

○ 2. WEDNESDAY

○ 3. THURSDAY

○ 4. FRIDAY

○ 5. SATURDAY / 6. SUNDAY

Goals:

Action Steps:

September

09/07/20 to 09/13/20

○ 7. MONDAY

○ 8. TUESDAY

○ 9. WEDNESDAY

○ 10. THURSDAY

○ 11. FRIDAY

○ 12. SATURDAY / 13. SUNDAY

Goals:

Action Steps:

September

09/14/20 to 09/20/20

○ 14. MONDAY

○ 15. TUESDAY

○ 16. WEDNESDAY

○ 17. THURSDAY

○ 18. FRIDAY

○ 19. SATURDAY / 20. SUNDAY

Goals:

Action Steps:

September

09/21/20 to 09/27/20

○ 21. MONDAY

○ 22. TUESDAY

○ 23. WEDNESDAY

○ 24. THURSDAY

○ 25. FRIDAY

○ 26. SATURDAY / 27. SUNDAY

Goals:

Action Steps:

October 2020

Sunday	Monday	Tuesday	Wednesday	Thursday	Friday	Saturday
27	28	29	30	1	2	3
4	5	6	7	8	9	10
11	12 **COLUMBUS DAY U.S. THANKSGIVING DAY - CAN**	13	14	15	16	17
18	19	20	21	22	23	24
25	26	27	28	29	30	31 **HALLOWEEN**

September

09/28/20 to 10/04/20

○ 28. MONDAY

○ 29. TUESDAY

○ 30. WEDNESDAY

○ 1. THURSDAY

○ 2. FRIDAY

○ 3. SATURDAY / 4. SUNDAY

Goals:

Action Steps:

October

10/05/20 to 10/11/20

○ 5. MONDAY

○ 6. TUESDAY

○ 7. WEDNESDAY

○ 8. THURSDAY

○ 9. FRIDAY

○ 10. SATURDAY / 11. SUNDAY

Goals:

Action Steps:

October

10/12/20 to 10/18/20

○ 12. MONDAY

○ 13. TUESDAY

○ 14. WEDNESDAY

○ 15. THURSDAY

○ 16. FRIDAY

○ 17. SATURDAY/ 18. SUNDAY

Goals:

Action Steps:

October

10/19/20 to 10/25/20

○ 19. MONDAY

○ 20. TUESDAY

○ 21. WEDNESDAY

○ 22. THURSDAY

○ 23. FRIDAY

○ 24. SATURDAY / 25. SUNDAY

Goals:

Action Steps:

October

10/26/20 to 11/01/20

○ 26. MONDAY

○ 27. TUESDAY

○ 28. WEDNESDAY

○ 29. THURSDAY

○ 30. FRIDAY

○ 31. SATURDAY / 1. SUNDAY

Goals:

Action Steps:

November 2020

Sunday	Monday	Tuesday	Wednesday	Thursday	Friday	Saturday
1 *DAYLIGHT SAVINGS TIME ENDS*	2	3	4	5	6	7
8	9	10	11 *VETERAN'S DAY U.S. / REMEMBERANCE DAY - CAN*	12	13	14
15	16	17	18	19	20 *NATIONAL CHILD DAY / CIBER MONDAY*	21
22	23	24	25	26 *THANKSGIVING DAY U.S.*	27 *BLACK FRIDAY U.S.*	28
29 *FIRST SUNDAY ADVENT*	30	1	2	3	4	5

November

11/02/20 to 11/08/20

○ 2. MONDAY

○ 3. TUESDAY

○ 4. WEDNESDAY

○ 5. THURSDAY

○ 6. FRIDAY

○ 7. SATURDAY / 8. SUNDAY

Goals:

Action Steps:

November

11/09/20 to 11/15/20

○ 9. MONDAY

○ 10. TUESDAY

○ 11. WEDNESDAY

○ 12. THURSDAY

○ 13. FRIDAY

○ 14. SATURDAY / 15. SUNDAY

Goals:

Action Steps:

November

11/16/20 to 11/22/20

○ 16. MONDAY

○ 17. TUESDAY

○ 18. WEDNESDAY

○ 19. THURSDAY

○ 20. FRIDAY

○ 21. SATURDAY / 22. SUNDAY

Goals:

Action Steps:

November

11/23/20 to 11/29/20

○ 23. MONDAY

○ 24. TUESDAY

○ 25. WEDNESDAY

○ 26. THURSDAY

○ 27. FRIDAY

○ 28. SATURDAY/29. SUNDAY

Goals:

Action Steps:

December 2020

Sunday	Monday	Tuesday	Wednesday	Thursday	Friday	Saturday
29	30	1	2	3	4	5
6	7	8	9	10	11 *HANNUKAH*	12
13	14	15	16	17	18	19
20	21 *WINTER SOLTICE*	22	23	24 *CHRISTMAS EVE*	25 *CHRISTMAS DAY*	26 *BOXING DAY KWANZAA BEGINS*
27	28	29	30	31 *NEW YEAR'S EVE*	1 *NEW YEAR'S DAY KWANZAA ENDS*	2

November

11/30/20 to 12/06/20

○ 30. MONDAY

○ 1. TUESDAY

○ 2. WEDNESDAY

○ 3. THURSDAY

○ 4. FRIDAY

○ 5. SATURDAY / 6. SUNDAY

Goals:

Action Steps:

December

12/07/20 to 12/13/20

○ 7. MONDAY

○ 8. TUESDAY

○ 9. WEDNESDAY

○ 10. THURSDAY

○ 11. FRIDAY

○ 12. SATURDAY / 13. SUNDAY

Goals:

Action Steps:

December

12/14/20 to 12/20/20

○ 14. MONDAY

○ 15. TUESDAY

○ 16. WEDNESDAY

○ 17. THURSDAY

○ 18. FRIDAY

○ 19. SATURDAY / 20. SUNDAY

Goals:

Action Steps:

December

12/21/20 to 12/27/20

○ 21. MONDAY

○ 22. TUESDAY

○ 23. WEDNESDAY

○ 24. THURSDAY

○ 25. FRIDAY

○ 26. SATURDAY / 27. SUNDAY

Goals:

Action Steps:

2021

January
S	M	T	W	T	F	S
					1	2
3	4	5	6	7	8	9
10	11	12	13	14	15	16
17	18	19	20	21	22	23
24	25	26	27	28	29	30
31						

February
S	M	T	W	T	F	S
	1	2	3	4	5	6
7	8	9	10	11	12	13
14	15	16	17	18	19	20
21	22	23	24	25	26	27
28						

March
S	M	T	W	T	F	S
	1	2	3	4	5	6
7	8	9	10	11	12	13
14	15	16	17	18	19	20
21	22	23	24	25	26	27
28	29	30	31			

April
S	M	T	W	T	F	S
				1	2	3
4	5	6	7	8	9	10
11	12	13	14	15	16	17
18	19	20	21	22	23	24
25	26	27	28	29	30	

May
S	M	T	W	T	F	S
						1
2	3	4	5	6	7	8
9	10	11	12	13	14	15
16	17	18	19	20	21	22
23	24	25	26	27	28	29
30	31					

June
S	M	T	W	T	F	S
		1	2	3	4	5
6	7	8	9	10	11	12
13	14	15	16	17	18	19
20	21	22	23	24	25	26
27	28	29	30			

July
S	M	T	W	T	F	S
				1	2	3
4	5	6	7	8	9	10
11	12	13	14	15	16	17
18	19	20	21	22	23	24
25	26	27	28	29	30	31

August
S	M	T	W	T	F	S
1	2	3	4	5	6	7
8	9	10	11	12	13	14
15	16	17	18	19	20	21
22	23	24	25	26	27	28
29	30	31				

September
S	M	T	W	T	F	S
			1	2	3	4
5	6	7	8	9	10	11
12	13	14	15	16	17	18
19	20	21	22	23	24	25
26	27	28	29	30		

October
S	M	T	W	T	F	S
					1	2
3	4	5	6	7	8	9
10	11	12	13	14	15	16
17	18	19	20	21	22	23
24	25	26	27	28	29	30
31						

November
S	M	T	W	T	F	S
	1	2	3	4	5	6
7	8	9	10	11	12	13
14	15	16	17	18	19	20
21	22	23	24	25	26	27
28	29	30				

December
S	M	T	W	T	F	S
			1	2	3	4
5	6	7	8	9	10	11
12	13	14	15	16	17	18
19	20	21	22	23	24	25
26	27	28	29	30	31	

Notes

Notes

Notes

www.ingramcontent.com/pod-product-compliance
Lightning Source LLC
Chambersburg PA
CBHW081455220526
45466CB00008B/2659